That Guy™

HOPE Shift 2020

"By faith we understand that the worlds were framed by the word of God, so that the things which are seen were not made of things which are visible."

william d. winship

First Printing: 2020, That Guy Publications & Productions.

ISBN: 9781654171216
Imprint: Independently published by "That Guy"

That Guy - Hope Shift 2020

Table of Contents

Introduction

Much of Society has been duped, in other words they have been tricked into believing things that are not true. Hope Shift 2020 provides Godly insight as to what we need to do presently to Advance.

Societies have been reacting and submitting to fear and intimidation, Hope Shift presents an opportunity to recognize the cause of dysfunctional societies, and offer a cure. The medical, scientific and psychological professions have studied and identified the symptoms that exist, then based on those symptoms try to treat the identified disease. Hope Shift offers the CURE. That Guy (JESUS) is the cure to all disease and illness and what it takes to solve all of our problems. He promised that, "**If my people**, which are **called by my name**, shall humble themselves, pray and seek **my** face and turn from their wicked ways, then I will hear from heaven, and will heal their land."[1]

Illness and disease have a source, that source by design has been given permission to consume and kill, the antidote is Christ Jesus (That Guy). "The thief cometh not, but for to steal, and to kill, and to destroy: **I am come that they might have life, and that they might have *it* more abundantly**." [2]

Today much of society has been informed by media and news organizations. These venues have programed society to serve their wicked ways. The resulting failed culture promotes a wicked agenda, one that sadly tries to erase God and promoted self serving special interests that serve mammon, opposed to Godly ends that serve Jesus. This epidemic has created an ideal opportunity to thrive as a Christ Follower. It is clearly our call to shine a flood light into wicked places.

---

[1] 2 Chronicles 7:14 King James Version (KJV)

[2] John 10:10 KJV

For centuries we have been merely treating symptoms, rather than finding the cause. The epic failure that tries to treat symptoms is our opportunity to present solutions that will redeem families, businesses and create healthy organizations that are driven by scripture.

We are witnessing a global awakening, one filled with unprecedented opportunity. The advantage we hold is our Bible, our Lord and our Faith. We must pick up our sword and fight, our weapons are more powerful than those creating havoc.

Humility and compassion is at the heart of this HOPE Shift, a global call to action, the momentum of the Lord that operates with a pure heart and righteous power. We are in a battle to win, to win souls ultimately to Christ. During this time, we also can enjoy the spoils of this battle, that being the redemptive, resurrection power we possess.

Practically we know that current marketing psychology even at an elite level has been based off psychological understandings of man created solutions, we are now in a season where we exercise faith that promotes pure hearted missions, faith that aligns with righteous power from heaven above. The virus that has caused social fear and dysfunction is being exposed. We can no longer allow defective influencers to manipulate our minds and stir anxiety. *"Current top sales psychology says that people will do 2 1/2 times more to avoid pain than to do what creates sustaining results."* Hope Shift 2020, is a pathway to turn to an Almighty God, and to create faith filled solutions.

Hope Shift 2020 is written at a time where HOPE has been tested, and genuine faith has become our new mandate. At the present moment society has entered a state of paralysis due to the Corona virus, this virus is not the cause of our dysfunction, it is the result of years of negligence, and exposes our lack of preparedness. At present the interest rates have been reduced to zero percent, people are looking to government to supply their needs, and Jesus is the only real HOPE.

We are at a crossroad where every reader will need to decide and take actions. This book provides you with the tools and resources needed to advance. We Christians are at the crescendo of advantage, the tipping point for those of us who believe and trust the Lord Jesus Christ.

cre·scen·do

/krəˈSHenˌdō/

*the loudest point reached in a gradually increasing sound."the port engine's sound **rose to a crescendo**" the highest point reached in a progressive increase of intensity."the hysteria **reached a crescendo** around the spring festival"*

Making the SHIFT, requires action and attention to the times we are in, we no longer can place our FAITH in Wall Street, and now will need to turn our attention to Main Street. While Wall Street most likely will recover, it is Main Street that will require your efforts and focused attention. What is happening currently is simply a WAKE UP call from heaven, one that requires us to make different choices. The Amazon monster, the Walmart and other such conglomerations have taken the Lion Share of the marketplace away from the little guy. Corporate greed is being exposed, and with that exposure lies opportunities. Let me suggest that in this time, you want to be the little guy. Remember it was David, a little guy that took down the Giant, Goliath.

As I am presently writing, I received the following TEXT:

“Italy had 250 deaths in one day - just a few days ago the highest deaths of any country … Yesterday they beat the record with 328 deaths in one day. This is crazy, God is in control but we are goin tot have to really look to Him. I don’t think most people are aware as to what is happening of how it will change lives and business concerns”

Humility is the precursor of all kinds of promotion, we are in a time where the humble will indeed inherit the earth. ***The Corona Virus will come and go, but the impact will be brutal to those who have not put on the full armor of God and recognized that this battle ends well for those of us who dare to shift into real hope, be real leaders, be really submitted to the Lordship of Jesus Christ, and associate with real Friends, those who remain diligent, vigilant and walk in harmony with heaven.*** Let this book be your call to action.

Who is That Guy?

The foundational question both men and women struggle with today is in their identity, their need to belong, and how to live with a sense of purpose. 'That Guy' solves those struggles immediately.

Rather than belabor this point lets identify who that guy is. In two words we will solve every current problem and all social, economic and political issues. Ready? ‘That Guy” is **Jesus Christ.**

Now that we know who ‘That Guy’ is, our goal is to help you shape a business model that is eternal and promotes practical ideas. ‘That Guy’ is the catalyst of change that will help you gain practical insights to improve your life, the lives of those you love, all while helping you intentionally form meaningful communities.

I want to take a brief moment to share with you the REAL story of how 'That Guy' became a business while painting a clear picture. A tangible blueprint and insight into this business model and how it brought us back to our roots while pushing forwards. With real movement comes friction that creates traction and momentum.

Transformation is hard work, moving from the familiar to full throttle faith is how That Guy was birthed! The majority of the time when something new is going to be born we experience adversity. Consultants are often their own worst enemy. We have “advice and ideas” that work, unfortunately, we tend to get so busy helping others we lose sight of the need to help ourselves. In the busyness of life, we tend to overlook our own need to employ the kinds of resources and strategies we offer our clients.

In my endeavors of writing books, creating a curriculum and helping others, I went broke. So broke in fact, that in a state of desperation I tried to sustain our life by being an UBER driver, a business model that works for UBER and it’s client but does not benefit the drivers because after you consider the insurance, taxes, gas, wear and tear on your automobile, it just might cost you money to drive. In this time I was low on cash flow but rich within Relationship, Faith, and a will to build something beyond myself. I looked at my bank account and it had -$7.77! Yes, negative; later that night meeting a friend of mine who ironically asked me to mentor him in business. So we both began driving, each making $50, just enough to launch 'That Guy'.

POINT being, you do not need capital to start a business, you just need to start!!!

The next morning my friend, John asked, “So what are we doing today?”

This is our true story about how we started a business with less than zero dollars and built this grass roots movement in such a short period. Through implementing hard work, focused effort and conscious strategy we created a well oiled grass roots machine. Leaving my professional consulting career of 18 years we joined along to embody the Blue Collar Boom MOVEMENT. Now we are enlisting other like minded individuals and giving them the proper tools by developing ‘That Guy’ franchises (FUNCHISES) driven and for our committed alliance members. We don’t aim to take part but redefine what it takes to be within industry driven by absolute truth. Having taught as a professional business consultant I'm blessed to have built foundations within elite tactics, practices, and networks. Hope Shift 2020 is the basic foundation towards a healthy expectation and proven direction. We Build Together.

This book will provide key principles, I call these concepts the BASIC FUNDAMENTALS needed to operate. Hope Shift is both practical and strategic. The concepts work in your personal and professional life, ONLY when applied.

We hope that this book will point you to the GREATEST Marketer, brander, and enterprise leader of all time, Jesus Christ (That Guy). He is the ultimate catalyst of consciousness.

This book contains proven knowledge and provides tested guidance so that you will achieve Profit by Design. “Profit by Design” includes developing a culture of excellence that reflect solid behavioral values that fully integrate with practical actionable standards. Profit is intentional, we have to shift out of hope and into ACTION. Action precedes TRACTION. You will discover the tools we used as a consulting firm, and be given direction valuable to your personal and professional achievements. Application promotes what we call the **Triple win - you win, those you serve win and the greater**

community around you win as well. NOT only that, you will cause a ripple, a ripple that changes the world. To those SERIOUS about gaining traction, purchase the book "Traction" by Gino Wickman and download the tool box https://www.eosworldwide.com/dl-tools/

For we are His workmanship, created in Christ Jesus for good works, which God prepared beforehand so that we would walk in them.

(NASB Ephesians 2:10)

Illustration 0.0 Strategy that causes Advantage has direction. The "Golden Blueprints" below provide the essentials. Behavioral Values, Principled Mindsets and Focused Efforts are the engineering used by high achievers. Consider the Golden Blueprints the GPS (God's Positional System)

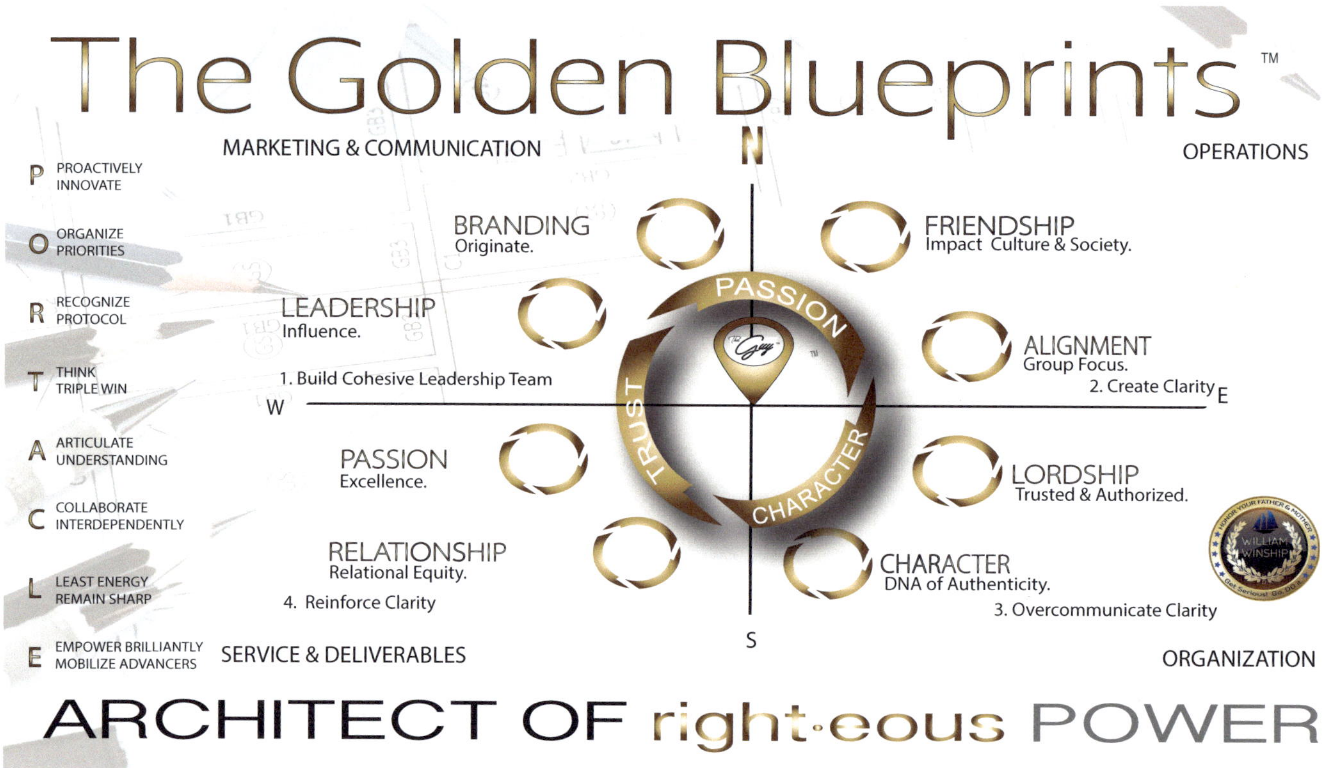

Neutral - HOPE Shift

Hope is Neutral, it is the center of everything else. Hope inspires vision, vision manifests as we intentionally recognize that for any great thing to happen, it must be inspired by real HOPE that is activated resulting in FAITH. The objective is to SHIFT into ACTION, to get real sustainable TRACTION. ***"If you could get all the people in an organization rowing in the same direction, you could dominate any industry, in any market, against any competition, at any time."***[3]

Now faith is the substance of things hoped for, the evidence of things not seen. Hebrew 11:1.[4]

Notice on the "Golden Blueprints" we start at the center. I like to think of this center as the scope on a Gun. Each day we all start off the same, having to awaken to the life we have created and look through this scope to determine the targets we must complete for each day. (What we HOPE to accomplish for each day, then pull the trigger and take down those giants, one at a time.)

HOPE is not just a word, it comes with real TANGIBLE results. Let's explore these passages.

Now faith is the substance of things hoped for, the evidence of things not seen.

-Hebrew 11:1.

Hope deferred makes the heart sick, but a longing fulfilled is a tree of life.

-Proverbs 13:12.

Wisdom is the principal thing; therefore get wisdom: and with all thy getting get understanding.

-Proverbs 4:7

And if one prevail against him, two shall withstand him; and a threefold cord is not quickly broken.

-Ecclesiastes 4:12

---

[3] Wickman, Gino. Traction (p. 30). BenBella Books, Inc.. Kindle Edition.

[4] Bible - King James Version

That Guy - Hope Shift 2020

Hope and Change were the essentials on which Barack Obama founded his campaign to become President of the United States. The issue with his Presidency was that while hope and change are essential, it must be clearly defined and ACTION taken toward those objectives. Sadly, Mr. Obama did not have a clear view for the American people to embrace, or to understand. Although, we Honor him for serving our nation, and the good efforts that he accomplished. In short, his presidency was confusing and did not engage the people. There is no doubt, he had a passion, and truly wanted to improve our nation, what he lacked was the engagement of people.

Fast forward to 2020, President Donald J. Trump has been in the cross fire of the democrats, threatened and impeached. The defining factors for Donald J. Trump is that even during the process of impeachment, he continues to focus on the objective, Making America Greater. He has provided the American people with a clear vision with hope for the future and has taken strategic action to see this vision come to fruition. His vision for the American people is laid out in this statement he made, "The forgotten men and women of our country will be forgotten no longer. The time for empty talk is over. Now arrives the hour for action. From this day forward, a new vision will govern our Land. From this day forward, it's going to be only "America First". - Donald J. Trump" Essentially, he is returning the power back to the people.

While Trump clearly has defined his mandate, the Democrats continue to plow forward with a "social, political and economic" agenda that is confusing at best. Perhaps it is the greatest assault ever to our democracy. Time will prove that Donald J. Trump will cause a "Trump Awakening". Waking up our nation to the essentials of what TRUE Hope and Change are about. He is aligned with God, as his values agree with the foundational truths which formed our Nation. He will be remembered as the best President America has ever known. As of NOW, the BLUE COLAR BOOOOM has begun. This book is your roadmap to doing GREATER things. (Gods Idea)

Now faith is the substance of things hoped for, the evidence of things not seen.
-Hebrew 11:1.

What are you HOPING for?

Name 10 things that you hope for, prioritize them in the in order of importance:

1)

2)

3)

4)

5)

6)

7)

8)

9)

10)

This book is a companion to my book WinSHIFT- The Advisors. In WinSHIFT I describe the concepts of business through Aviation. In this book, I provide a dashboard that contains the tools to win in life and to become a great enterprise leader who Profits by Design. Think of this book as the essentials, and consider WinShift as the application or workbook. This book will help you apply your learning with the ultimate goal of continuous improvement and the development of high yielding enterprise leaders.

I felt compelled to add an illustration utilized in Aviation to draw your attention to the need to SHIFT - bad habits need to be replaced by exceptional habits, those that promote profitable futures. In the illustration below you can easily understand how attitudes and behavior shape your destination and destiny.

Illustration 1.0 In Aviation as in life we have RULES of engagement that every champion would be wise to consider & apply. The following illustration describes the diligence needed to engineer a safe flight and how to apply this to real life. Aviation provides a pathway for safe power or righteous power. When we allow our attitudes to align with the “rules” or principles of enterprise maturity - things tend to work.

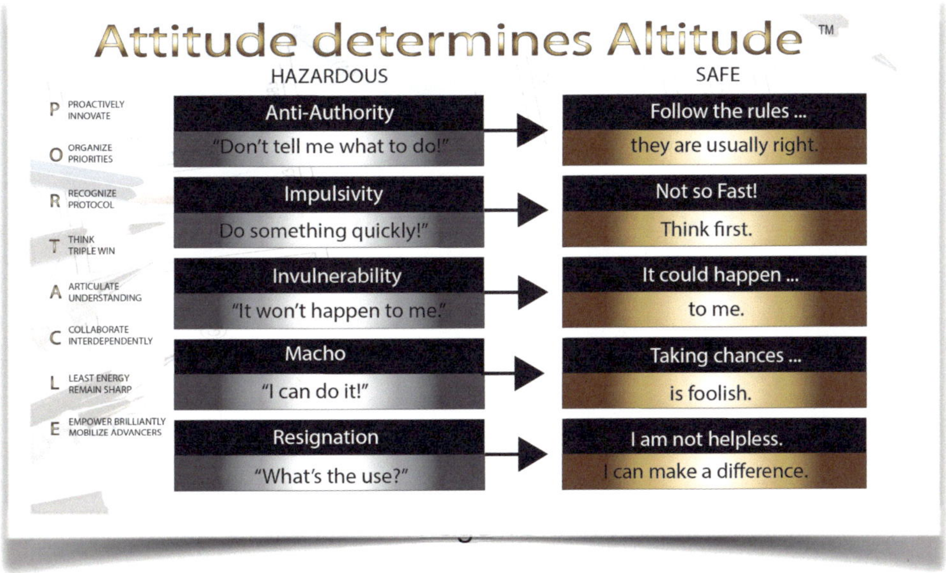

Illustration 2.0 This is the FIRST quadrant of the Golden Blueprints. The Golden Blueprints are part of a larger bodied work we have developed to train Enterprise Leaders. In the first quadrant we focus on the development of "Cohesive Leadership Teams" through the development of Influence Leaders that represent their brand with excellence.

First Gear - LEADER Shift - "Building Community"

Enterprise Leadership is not exclusive, it includes janitors, housewives, doctors, realtors and all such personalities which contribute to society in various ways. Leadership is a subject that has been written about, taught relentlessly and perhaps become a "subject of debate" for centuries. The fact is, EVERYONE is a leader, the challenge with this premise is that given this fact not everyone governs their life in a manner that considers the long view and ends well.

This book if the content is applied to your life it will promote a Leader SHIFT. Essentially this book promotes two major ideas; behavioral values to govern your life and culture as well key life principles designed to promote habits that create desirable results and optimal achievement.

This book was designed after 18 years of learning and discovering what works. When the principles and behavioral values are applied they together create a real shift on many levels that benefits those who have determined to win in life. Hope Shift 20/20 promotes the key principles and behaviors needed to lead, it is all about LEADER Shift. Leadership is modeled, true leadership is an action, activity and demonstration of competence that includes character. Trust is the END RESULT.

When leadership is put into action, it is noticed by others. True leadership will produce optimal results in behavior and activity. Changes in society, the economy, and spiritual conditions begin to manifest in society at large when leadership is put into action. Instead of viewing leadership from the sidelines, consider NOW that every great leader becomes great as a result of behaviors and key principles that allow that leader to LEAD through modeling, as opposed to just talk. The old cliche, "you talk the talk, but do you walk the walk" is appropriate. LEADER Shift includes standards that integrate with behavior. This book describes both.

Instead of trying to become a Leader, SHIFT Gears and decide you are one.

In the “Golden Blueprints”, we delve into the concept that once you decide to be a leader, absolutely everything you do, say, and model, contributes to who you are in life and forms your character. Your Brand is tied directly to your character. Character drives every aspect of your life.

In order to be a leader, one must be authentic. As a leader you need to ensure that your leadership and brand are congruent, which will result in a **Cohesive Leadership Team.**

In the book WinSHIFT, I describe an Algorithm as a mathematical formula to keep in mind as you endeavor to be successful both personally and professionally. In this “formula” the central idea of genuine leadership is to operate in right standing with God and others, we call this kind of optimal LEADER Shift RIGHTEOUS POWER. The best way to live an empowered life is to live life intentionally. The qualities that are needed to live this optimal life include, understanding, a pure heart, righteous power, wisdom, and favor.

The algorithm of high achievers is as follows: ***Understanding + A Pure Heart = Righteous Power = Wisdom + Favor***

The goal of LEADER Shift is to ultimately create communities that arise and establish cultures with Honor and Integrity. Authentic Cities or Authenticity.

Illustration 3.0 This is the SECOND quadrant of the Golden Blueprints. The Golden Blueprints are part of a larger body of work we have developed to train Enterprise Leaders. In the second quadrant, we focus on “Creating Clarity” through group focus that intentionally impacts culture & society with positive experiences.

Second Gear - FRIEND Shift -"Your Relationship with Others"

In business and management we may have been taught not to be friendly with the "workers". This kind of teaching is not necessarily working. In this chapter we align with the "Golden Blueprints". Our focus is to become a Cohesive TEAM. We become a "friend" to our colleagues, those we serve, and this ideal creates authentic communities. Pointing to the book WinSHIFT- The Advisors we discuss the concept of the "Triple Win". In an effort to win in life, everyone connected to you must win as well. This idea promotes that you win, those you serve will win and the work that you do has some kind of missional purpose so that the larger community around you wins as well. (Community Formation)

"Friendship" is an idea that may be foreign in management theory today because many families, organizations and businesses have not taken the time to develop deep meaningful relationships. In this chapter we hope to create a FRIEND Shift. (Relational Equity)

With no exception, being a friend will require that you are vulnerable. To be vulnerable in a healthy way often attracts true friends because most people want transparency and authenticity. The reason why it is hard to be friendly and genuine is because sometimes people can disappoint, betray, and even take advantage. FRIEND Shift requires that you develop a new mindset, keyed on thinking the best about others.

In the following scripture, it describes an ideal mindset and points to 'That Guy', God who fashioned every detail so that we could indeed be a true friend and friendly at the same time. **"He hath made every thing beautiful in his time: also he hath set the world in their heart, so that no man can find out the work that God taketh from the beginning to the end.** Ecclesiastes 3:11[5] Perhaps God's greater desire is to be your FRIEND.

---

[5] King James Version, The Bible.

Once you embrace the concept of having a culture that involves Friends working together, the practical aspects of "How To" come into play. While this idea may stretch you somewhat (or even a lot), it will be necessary to keep and maintain CLEAR parameters and definite boundaries so you remain in a state where FRIEND Shift is possible. Friends will respect the boundaries, and communities become healthy and prosperous as a result.

As an added value to this book, I feel compelled to provide you with a NEW concept of building a growing enterprise, it is the 'That Guy' Method. "That Guy" is engineered as an alliance that intentionally develops members of its team by working in agreement with "That Guy" (God) and others. We believe that every team member, every vendor that interacts with our clients needs to be in agreement or in alignment with our Brand, that being "That Guy". In order to accomplish this objective practically we created a document called "An Alliance Agreement" . This document outlines the ideals and understandings that are needed in order to establish **friendship based relationship** with those we closely associate. The "Alliance Agreement" is a foundational legal document from which we execute to enforce "Righteous Power" and maintain long term associations that "Profit by Design". (If you would like a copy of this agreement just email me at william@thatguy.co. The document is a template that you may wish to have your legal counsel review, revise and create specifically to suit your needs. It is the "Governing Document" that encourages Cohesive Teams.

The real FRIEND Shift includes rules of engagement so you will create healthy, stable and growing enterprises. Having clear objectives promotes high engagement and establishes expectations. Nothing clarifies expectations like the failure to meet them. Cohesive teams are dependent on clearly laid out objectives that are followed, these objectives are foundational to long term achievements.

The Goal of FRIEND Shift is to ultimately create cohesion among your colleagues, venders and clients. This set of guidelines applies directly to FRIEND Shift as we journey together to our next destination, RELATION Shift.

The algorithm of high achievers is as follows:

Understanding + A Pure Heart = Righteous Power = Wisdom + Favor

Third Gear - RELATION Shift - Your Behavior & Values"

Character is the sum total of how you personally and professionally show up and behave. Character is the DNA of an organization. Character leads with responsibility and is a discipline of Righteous Power (Safe Power).

Behavior is shaped by the implementation of habits that are formed intentionally and ensure that we have a template to follow; this was created as a result of learning from Steven Covey in his book, The Seven Habits of Highly Effective People. Essentially the idea of habit formation comes with the engineering of those habits around Passion, Trust, and Character.

Illustration 4.0 The 8 Standards are a template to remind you of the essentials that create High achievement, they are designed to ensure you develop optimal habits to win in life.

8 Standards - Principles or Habits of High Achievers

	Standard	Principle
P	PROACTIVELY INNOVATE	"Principles of personal vision, you are responsible for change."
O	ORGANIZE PRIORITIES	"Aligning Passion to Priorities - imagination of greater futures, and creating fresh scripts for life."
R	RECOGNIZE PROTOCOL	"Advance with discipline and model serving leadership that operates with authority and honors protocol at all times."
T	THINK TRIPLE WIN	*"Living authentically so that the long view is established. Form agreements based on serving, empowering others to serve, and Influencing those you serve with results that serve to empower and grow character."*
A	ARTICULATE UNDERSTANDING	"Listen deeply to understand the needs, desires and goals of others, then align persuasion with integrity to achieve optimal relational excellence and team growth." aka Communication with Integrity and Character.
C	COLLABORATE INTERDEPENDENTLY	"Creative cooperation, ensuring that the total intellectual, emotional and passions of the team are understood before taking any actions."
L	LEAST ENERGY REMAIN SHARP	*"Key in on continuous improvement both personally and professionally. Remaining in a state of continuous improvement and developing high performance, requires that you remain diligent to excellence as the highest standard."*
E	EMPOWER BRILLIANTLY MOBILIZE ADVANCERS	"Long view considerations that produce results. Leaving a Legacy of Leadership™"

In the book, WinSHIFT- The

Advisors I Look at each principle and give insight as to why each principle is critical and how the principles work to help ensure that you personally and professionally shift from a position of letting life happen to you, to living life with intentionality and on purpose.

For me the REAL Shift that informs my life and the greater work that I do will always be “relational”. “Relational Equity” is developed and often produces material wealth as evidence that there is a true correlation to quality relationship and profitable enterprises. This theory was taught by David Maister as opposed to material rewards. (Rewards follow when “relational equity” is built)

Let me just pause here because you may need to understand WHY Relational equity is primary. Relational Equity AND Material Rewards are important. Both drive Profit by Design, yet the relational equity must be present to win in the marketplace.

Below I provide a diagram that is used as a metric or standard, developed by a great business scholar (David Maister) This diagram essentially promotes the building of High Equity Relationships. In his book, Practice what you preach, David promotes the following: “Financial performance is driven by quality and client relationships. Quality and client relationships are driven by employee satisfaction. Employee satisfaction is driven by high standards, coaching and empowerment. High standards are driven by fair compensation and commitment, enthusiasm, and respect. Coaching is driven by long-term orientation and commitment, enthusiasm, and respect. Empowerment is driven by long-term orientation.” [6]

In Maisters diagram, he proves that RELATIONSHIPS DRIVE PROFIT, I call this concept, “Profit by Design”.

[6] Maister, David H.. Practice What You Preach: What Managers Must Do To Create A High Achievement Culture (p. 84). Free Press. Kindle Edition.

Maister, David H. (2001-10-18). Practice What You Preach: What Managers Must Do To Create A High Achievement Culture

DO THE MATH

Let me explain why Material Wealth has a direct correlation to Relational Equity; I like stuff, I enjoy rewards. So much so, I make it my job to reward myself with new stuff every time I can. Alternatively, I believe in rewarding people, those we associate with, giving them gifts for good behavior is a reasonable service. Incentives drive profit and prove our commitment to others.

Unapologetically, I intentionally surround myself with the "BEST", best cars, best tools, best technology, and especially best people. The naysayer might get the impression I am all about material wealth yet that would be a misunderstanding. Work produced those things, and it brings me great joy to have nicer things. As an example, I prefer to fly "Delta ONE" First Class because it is comfortable in the sofa seats, the service is extreme and once in a while, I have the BEST Flight Attendant in the World, serving me. Her name is Cherie Winship, the BEST wife, and BEST Flight attendant in the World.

I am boasting because I know the source of the greater things is God, for that reason I give him the Glory for providing me with the BEST. In the next chapter we will explore more about "That Guy" but for now let's consider the primary focus of this chapter, RELATION Shift.

The 8 Principles will form your behavior, while behavioral values form the quality you create as they relate to the "Culture" of your organization, enterprise, and personal life. The core behavioral values consist of Character, Trust, and Passion but we have added a few more to ensure that the attributes that guide an organization, business and your personal life are well rounded. Fun was added because balance is essential. Honor was added because when we honor others we tend to develop healthy cultures. I added Kindness because when we behave in a manner that is kind we are able to bring about higher results with others. When were are genuinely kind, we develop power with others, opposed to power over others. Finally, Humility because I wanted to differentiate between a false sense of humility and one that is real. Real "Authentic" Humility is courageous and confident and pays the cost that others do not.

On the next pages I have listed the behavioral values. In my personal operational center I have an oval table that I call my "I AM Table". Each chair has an imbedded behavioral value. I have 8 chairs at the table, 7 chairs contain the Behavioral values, the last chair at the head of the table is the "Golden

Blueprint". The best part of this table is that it can also be used as a white board, so I have dry erase markers I use to keep notes and allow others to make notes as we develop ideas, strategies needed to collaborate, innovate and mobilize. It is a boardroom of sorts. I actually consider the table as the Engine or wisdom center from which we build. It is where creative ideas and strategy connect and get executed.

Illustration 5.0 This is the THIRD quadrant of the Golden Blueprints. The Golden Blueprints are part of a larger body of work we have developed to train Enterprise Leaders. In the third quadrant we focus to "Reinforce Clarity". We establish Excellence as the STANDARD, being ultimately the BRAND or Character of business, organization, and your personal growth. **The BRAND & Culture is the Character** (sum TOTAL of behavior, values & standards). The Brand is the best reviled as you develop culture. The Character or Culture (Brand) is maintained by established systems, controls, and incentives that are followed with absolute discipline to ensure integrity, TRUE INTEGRITY. (Authenticity)

CHARACTER

Is the DNA of an Organization

Leads with RESPONSIBILITY

Is a DISCIPLINE of:

SAFE POWER

Has Authority & Accountability

HONOR

AWARENESS of other's talent

Respect and APPRECIATION

Seeing VALUE in others

AFFIRMING

Raising OTHERS up

TRUST

Is DEVELOPED
and a product of INTEGRITY

Is DRIVEN by:

ACTION & BEHAVIOR

Costs, when you compromise

FUN

Enjoyable WORK

CELEBRATING achievements

Laughing TOGETHER

a sincere SMILE.

JOYFUL & AMUSING

PASSION

When you are most ALIVE

Abiding in PURPOSE

Remaining FAITHFUL

RISKING everything

KNOWING it's worth it

KIND

Is GENEROUS

expressed through GRATITUDE

OTHERS centered.

EMPATHETIC & SUPPORTIVE

WARM - HEARTED

HUMILITY

Not a lack of COURAGE

Requires CONFIDENCE

Is a RESULT of:

LOVING SERVICE

Pays the COST others DON'T

Overdrive - LORD Shift - "Your Relationship with God"

No SERMON needed. This gets personal, it is the relationship you hold with the Creator of the Universe. "That Guy" has a NAME, a Name above all names. His Name is POWER and gives us the ABILITY to Grow. "That Guy" is the BEST BRAND, it is better than Coca Cola. While Coca Cola touts that they are the "REAL THING", 'That Guy' is the genuine article. His name is Jesus Christ, in-fact the version I know, is "That Guy, No Other Name". In the first part of this book I referred to a sequence of scriptures, one of which is "And if one prevail against him, two shall withstand him; and a three fold cord is not quickly broken." Ecclesiastes 4:12. The 3rd cord is "That Guy" Jesus Christ. When you include and give credit to HIM, all things are possible. The question that will ultimately need to be reconciled is; "Is Jesus Christ your Lord?" Does he honestly own everything including your Heart? Have you determined to honor HIM with EVERYTHING? That is the LORD Shift, being all in.

For I, the LORD your God, will hold your **right hand**, saying to you, 'Fear not, I will help you.

One name
Holds weight above them all
His fame
Outlasts the Earth He formed
His praise
Resounds beyond the stars
And echoes in our hearts
The greatest One of all
His face
Shines brighter than the sun

His grace
As boundless as His love
He reigns
With healing in His wings
The King above all kings
The greatest One of all
Lift up our eyes
See the King has come
Light of the world
Reaching out for us
There is no other name
There is no other name
Jesus Christ our God, oh oh oh
Seated on high
The undefeated One
Mountains bow down
As we lift Him up
There is no other name
There is no other name
Jesus Christ our God, whoa oh oh oh
Find hope

That Guy - Hope Shift 2020

When all the world seems lost
Behold
The triumph of the cross
His power
Has trampled death and grave
Our life found in His name
The greatest name of all
Lift up our eyes
See the King has come
Light of the world
Reaching out for us
There is no other name
There is no other name
Jesus Christ our God, oh oh oh
Seated on high
The undefeated One
Mountains bow down
As we lift Him up
There is no other name
There is no other name

That Guy - Hope Shift 2020

Jesus Christ our God, oh oh oh
Jesus
The Earth will shake
And tremble before Him
Chains will break
As Heaven and Earth sing
Holy is the name
Holy is the name of
Jesus, Jesus, Jesus
The Earth will shake
And tremble before Him
Chains will break
As Heaven and Earth sing
Holy is the name
Holy is the name of
Jesus, Jesus, Jesus
Lift up our eyes, see the King has come
Light of the world reaching out for us
There is no other name
There is no other name
Jesus Christ our God, oh oh oh

That Guy - Hope Shift 2020

Seated on high, the undefeated One
Mountains bow down as we lift Him up
There is no other name
There is no other name
There is no other name
There is no other name
Jesus Christ [7]

Focus Produces "Profit by Design"

---

[7] No Other Name - Lyric - Hillsong Worship

Illustration 6.0 This is the FOURTH quadrant of the Golden Blueprints. The Golden Blueprints are part of a larger body of work we have developed to train Enterprise Leaders. In the final quadrant we focus to "Over-communicate Clarity" **An algorithm of high achievers is as follows:** ***Understanding x A Pure Heart = Righteous Power = Wisdom x Favor.*** The whole point is that God's Word is the foundation for any Great Enterprise, Organization, Marriage or empowered Life. The concepts that create REAL change or Shifts in your life are originated by the Word of God, who spoke everything into being, including this book.

HOPE SHIFT Epilog

Finally, my brethren, be strong in the Lord, and in the power of his might. Ephesians 6:10[8]

Faith is the substance (Provision) of the things Hoped for (Vision), the evidence (Material Things & Relational Equity) of things not seen. Hope deferred makes the heart sick, (where we can get stuck) but a longing fulfilled is a tree of life. (Abundance - The proof) Wisdom is the principal thing; (Most Important) therefore get wisdom: (Take Action) and with all thy getting get understanding. (Continuous Improvement, don't quit) And if one prevail against him, (We have ONE enemy) two can withstand him; (Accountability) and a threefold cord is not quickly broken. (LORD Shift). Include the Lord in all you do and follow that still small voice. AS I Complete his book, I looked at the clock, it is January 1, 2020, at exactly 1:11PM, with its final edit completed at 2:22 PM on 2/2/2020.

With that, Enjoy this Journey, and Praise God for the Advantage!

ACTS 20:20

"And now I kept nothing back from you, but have shewed you, and have taught you publicly, and from house to house, and that I've not held anything back from you that would help you grow."

The Transition has happened, the Shift is in operation, and now it's time to Accelerate. You are destined to Shift into ALL God has for you in 2020. CLEAR vision and victory is upon you.

Blessings "That Guy"

[8] Kings James Version

Golden GRATITUDE Shifts - 10 Things I am GRATEFUL for

1.

2.

3.

4.

5.

6.

7.

8.

9.

10.

Assignment: Keep this list with you every day, Thank God for these items every morning and every night This one assignment will advance you beyond hope, to a place where your faith is engaged.

Why should we give thanks to God?

- God created everything, and He created it good. 1 Timothy 4:4-5. ...
- God made us, and we are His people. Psalm 100:3. ...
- God's love for us never ceases. 1 Chronicles 16:34. ...
- God freely **gives** us His grace. 1 Corinthians 1:4. ...
- God satisfies our every need. Psalm 107:8-9.

Illustration 7.0 At the center you have a clearly defined why as the leading edge or epicenter of your enterprise. Around the "Prop" you have a team of people who operate with character, they have a clear path or process that works together around a product you believe in. The competitive vector helps to remind us that we must continue to improve and keep an eye on Quality, Cost, and Exclusivity as we build our enterprise.

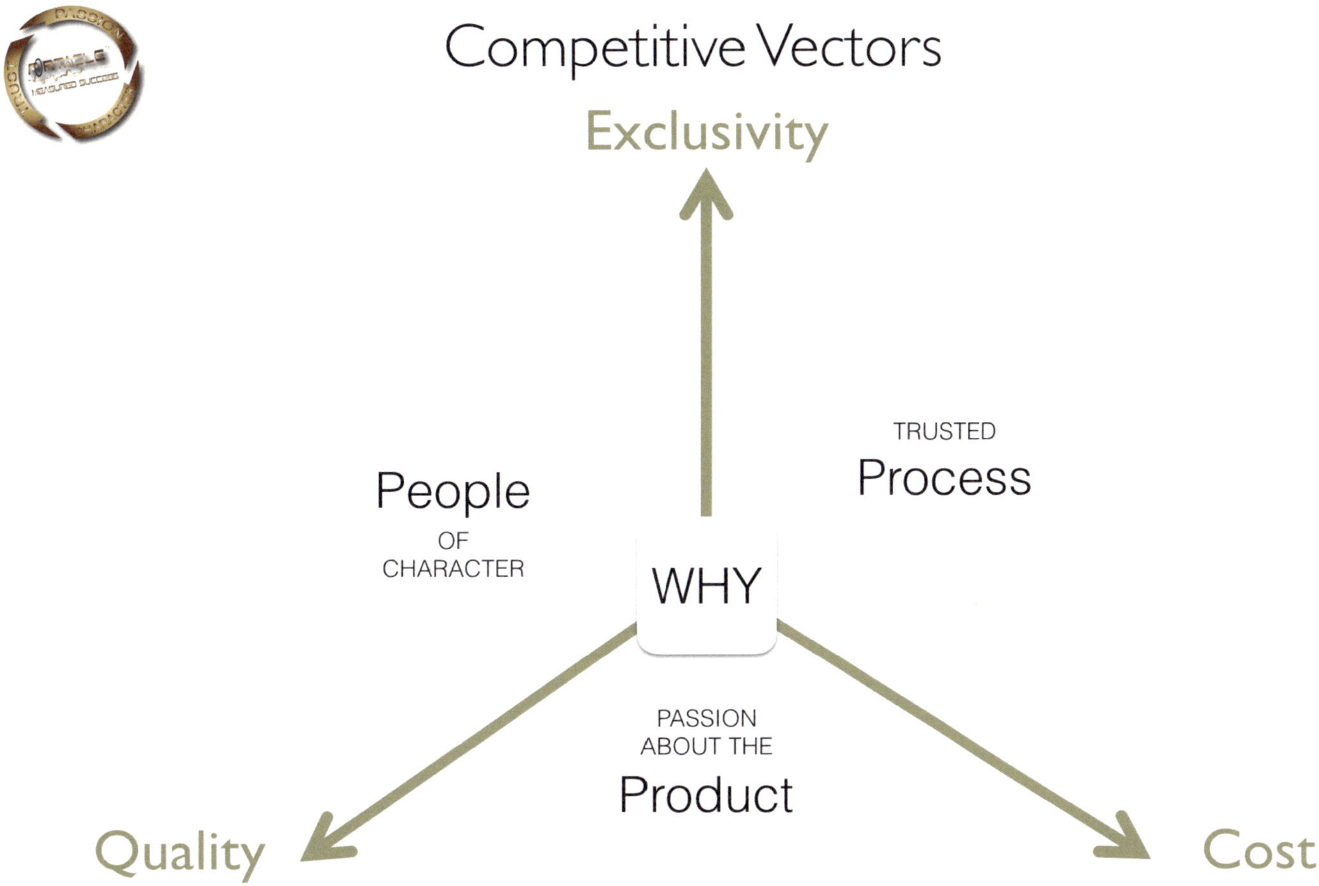

Illustration 8.0 Conflict in life is certain, below is what we call the conflict resolution wheel, it when properly followed helps to reduce/resolve conflicts.

Philemon Tree of Life Version (TLV)

Greetings to a House Group
1 Paul, a prisoner of Messiah *Yeshua*, and Timothy our brother, to Philemon our beloved and fellow worker.
2 To Apphia our sister, to Archippus our fellow soldier, and to the community that meets in your house:
3 Grace to you and *shalom* from God our Father and the Lord Messiah *Yeshua*!

Thanks for Love and Comfort

4 I thank my God always when mentioning you in my prayers, **5** hearing of your
love and the trust you have toward the Lord *Yeshua* and all the *kedoshim*. **6** May
the fellowship of your faith become effective, with the recognition of all the good
that is ours in Messiah. **7** For I've received much joy and comfort in your love,
brother, because the hearts of the *kedoshim* have been refreshed through you.

Request for Philemon's Runaway

8 Therefore, though I have plenty of boldness in Messiah to order you to do
what's right, **9** yet for love's sake I appeal to you instead. I, Paul, am an old man
and now also a prisoner belonging to Messiah *Yeshua*. **10** I beg you for my child
Onesimus—for whom I became a spiritual father while in chains. **11** He once
was useless to you, but now is useful both to you and me. **12** I sent him back to
you—he is my very heart. **13** I really wanted to keep him with me, so that on
your behalf he might serve me while I am in chains for the Good News. **14** But I
didn't want to do anything without your consent, so that your goodness

wouldn't be by force but by free will. **15** For perhaps he was separated from you
for a while in order that you might have him back forever, **16** no longer as a slave
but more than a slave—as a beloved brother, especially to me but even more so
to you, both in the flesh and in the Lord. **17** So if you consider me a partner,
welcome him as you would welcome me. **18** But if he has done you any wrong
or owes you anything, charge that to my account. **19** I, Paul, am writing this with
my own hand: I will repay. (Not to mention that you owe me your very
self.) **20** Yes, brother, let me have some benefit from you in the Lord. Refresh my
heart in Messiah.

Added Request and Farewell

21 Having confidence in your obedience, I write to you, knowing that you will do
even more than what I say. **22** At the same time also, prepare a guest room for
me—for I hope that through your prayers I will be given back to
you. **23** Epaphras, my fellow prisoner in Messiah *Yeshua*, greets you. **24** So do
Mark, Aristarchus, Demas, and Luke, my fellow workers. **25** May the grace of
our Lord Messiah *Yeshua* be with your spirit. Amen.

The book of Philemon is the ULTIMATE Business Plan for both Ministry and Enterprise Expansion.

Let me explain…

Paul was incarcerated (in jail for a crime he did not commit), while he was in Jail he met Onesimus (A fugitive, a thief and one great mess). In business one of the key frustrations is that the employer (Slave Driver) can not find good employees (Slaves). Paul by permission mentored Onesimus, and with a pure heart helped him to be FULLY restored to the person that Onimus stole from, that being the KING (Philemon). In-FACT he promoted him from a thief to a PARTNER or included MEMBER.

Interestingly, this slave's name Onesimus meant that he was "beneficial and profitable". Provision always comes with clarity and once understood and implemented provides great physical, spiritual and eternal rewards. In the book of Philemon, the run away slave was mentored by Paul, commissioned and sent back to the King with a mandate (Mission to influence and restore others). He was transformed from a thief (TAKER) then equalized with the King to be profitable (GIVER). Interestingly the name Philemon means Affectionate or one who kisses. Essentially Paul who lead Philemon to the saving knowledge of Jesus Christ dedicated an epistle (love letter) to the one who kisses. It was a kiss of LIFE, allowing the King an opportunity to expand the great work that Paul encourages.

This book promotes God's Business model, one of restoration and prosperity. This book contains business tools that include persuasion, negotiation, righteous use of the equity (relational equity) in relationships, accountability, values, and vision. Essentially the book of Philemon sets a STANDARD. The high standard promotes an excellent culture while offering a healthy communication style to encourage righteous behavior so that the "Church" (Ethics & Morals) AND "Enterprise" (Production & Profit) work to serve the greater community.

The conversation appealed to the heart of the King, empowering the king to make righteous choices. ***Understanding x A Pure Heart = Righteous Power = Wisdom x Favor.***

From my Intercessor

Everyone in life needs prayer. It is foundational to any enterprise, organization, marriage or family. I asked Judith (my intercessor) to provide a final word over the manuscript, one that promotes the essence of this work, she did an amazing Job. I also thank my friend Alisa for her energy and devotion to this work, she edits and fills the gaps of the pages to translate my ideas with clarity. I thank you both. I dedicate this to my wife Cherie who stands with me during the adverse times and enjoys the fruit of our efforts. A Three fold cord is not easily broken, although it may get torn and tattered at times, we trust "That Guy".

Romans 12:11,12
Be enthusiastic to serve the Lord, keeping your passion toward him boiling hot! Radiate with the glow of the Holy Spirit and let him fill you with excitement as you serve him. Let this hope burst forth within you, releasing a continual joy.

It is so incredible to watch people that glow with joy. They don't have to say a word! You look into their eyes and they tell a story that you'd love to hear! It's as if they have a secret that is bursting on the inside of them. Excitement and passion are good words to describe how they live. Nothing is ordinary or boring because of the life that they carry within them. That life is Jesus Christ, their Lord and Savior, and they walk in joy because the Holy Spirit gives them hope.

This book is about 'That Guy'--the one that gives deep and genuine life. You might know Him already but if not, let this book be an introduction and encourage you to move in hope and joy.

Judith Oldridge

Made in the USA
Columbia, SC
07 December 2023

27977198R00029